The Blouse & Skirt Handbook:

Book 2 of the Stylish Upgrades Series
find the hidden JOY in your wardrobe

2017
By Suze Solari

Table of Contents

Dedication

To my lovely husband Joe, whose tech expertise & indie publishing knowledge was invaluable in completing this project.

And he always wears what I tell him to!

You can learn more about Suze at www.suzesolaristyle.com.

TEXT Blouse to 44222 and get bonus video content and flat lays for FREE!

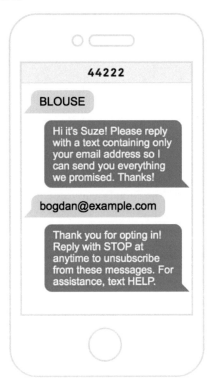

Having a wardrobe that we love helps us to feel expressive and confident. It also allows others to see us in our most radiant state. A great wardrobe gets us out of hiding. We stop wasting energy "figuring out what to wear" and can use that energy enjoying ourselves and creating lives we love.

Suze loves helping others feel confident so they can easily show up and do great work in the world. She removes the wardrobe obstacles that are in the way of her clients being seen for their true powerful selves.

Suze is a great model of what it looks like to confidently explore your own style in her writing, videos and her private work. In ninety-minutes she completely re-sparked an interest in me to feel and look good in my clothes, that I had lost 10 years ago.

This is how Suze helped me:

- Saved me a few hundred dollars $$$$ by seeing some of my clothes in a new way so now I will keep them instead of getting rid of them.
- Saved me hundreds more by telling me what I need to buy to round out my wardrobe rather than me buying random shit anytime I torturously get to a store.
- Got me creatively inspired because I felt good about looking good again and seeing my style …. a mix between euro and athletic I suppose. Again, it inspired me to go look for items I really dig and not buy random items.
- Sent links to items – what a massive TIME

SAVER!!! She told me where to go.

- Told me what lines and shapes look good on me and which don't.
- Gave me links to simple makeup I can use quickly for Skype business calls.
- AND we laughed!!! She made it so easy and fun.
- This book is another example of her ability to guide others to find what works uniquely for them. Suze translates her passion for design to help you choose pieces that feel right for your own style.

CHOOSE to BE CURIOUS,

Kelly Sheets

WHO IS THIS BOOK FOR?

This book is written for the woman who wants to stand out – perhaps in a playful way, yet as a strong individual, with confidence. Who knows she has a purpose to fulfill and may need a little help along the way to create an extraordinary life, with a wardrobe that reflects it. She is one who has conquered jeans, feels like she has it down – and is now ready to add a new look, a more feminine aesthetic, to her repertoire.

My friends and most of the people I know think I am always over- dressed. I believe, however that a fantastic outfit is my special sauce, my amour if you will. My awesome outfits help me FEEL empowered, gifted, worthy and ready to achieve whatever I desire.

To tell you something interesting, these same friends now show up at our gatherings dressed just a little bit snappier, taking a few extra moments to make the effort because they knew they would be seeing me. "I wore this for you, Suze" are the comments I hear, and I can truly sense their happiness and excitement for how fabulous they feel!

This is why I wrote The Blouse and Skirt Handbook, as a sequel to <u>The T-Shirt and Jeans Handbook</u>. I wanted to help my clients andand friends demystify a big section of their wardrobes, that they are not wearing and to continue their journey, to creative self – expression, self – love and joy.

If you are interested in taking that next step, and like the look of skirts, but unsure of which ones flatter your body, then this is the book for you. Or how about what blouses to pair with them, and how to complete the look? We will cover that too, and all along the way show you how fashion and style can be fun, and provide a vital role in not just looking amazing, but being amazing.

SECTION ONE: INTRODUCTION

"Give a girl the right shoes, and she can conquer the world"
Bette Midler

The way you choose to dress yourself completely affects the way you feel and then contributes to the results you get. I'm sure you've noticed that when you feel confident, powerful, sexy, radiant, you show up so much more in every moment. You speak your mind, dance wilder, ask for what you want - - that confidence radiates out into the world, and you make a great impression!

I know this to be true, and my goal with this book, just as

with every person I work with, is to help you tap into that most authentic and amazing expression of yourself. This expression of loving, kind, successful, and fun is achieved by knowing what clothes will light you up and how you can start creating that for yourself every single day.

With my first book, the T-Shirt and Jeans Handbook - I wanted to start at the beginning: to be a resource for everyday women who have lost their style along the way and want it back. A t-shirt and jeans is the daily uniform for countless women. In that look-book I provide resources to elevate the t-shirt and jeans look to something special. With easy, step-by-step instructions, I show how a basic outfit can be quickly transformed into a comfortable, chic and timeless look for almost any occasion. Also provided are fit guidelines for every body shape, as well as shopping resources to help you refresh your T-shirt and jeans wardrobe.

Why Blouse and Skirts?

Every woman has a few of these garments in their closet, and sometimes wonder how to wear them, or are bored with the same old look they put together. This handbook, like the first in the series, is intended to give you the creative inspiration to continue your path to stylish comfort and add in additional garment types that support your style.

I'm a firm believer in effortless dressing that supports the true nature of your individual style. The right fitting clothes can make every outfit cooler and every trend more manageable. The most modern, flattering blouses for your body type are unveiled here. The cut, fit and silhouette are the terms we will discuss for each blouse type, along with the fabric and how that affects the style and comfort of each garment.

Section Take-Aways

1. First impressions are lasting.

2. What you wear affects how you feel about yourself and how others treat you.

3. The blouse and skirt are the quintessential work and party uniform.

SECTION TWO: BODY TYPE

Matching body type to the most flattering cut of skirt and blouse:

In general, most of us know what looks best on us—what pieces we consistently gravitate toward, the ones that makes us feel confident. If you're not one of those people, read on this section provides an in-depth look at dressing for your body type, always an elevating endeavor.

There are so many garment silhouettes on the market, how is one supposed to successfully navigate through shopping and dealing with current trends for your specific body type?

Are you even sure of what your body type is?

To help you I am breaking down a few of the most common body shapes by definition. We will identify the areas you should be trying to accentuate, and which pieces to shop for that will help you do exactly that.

Perfectly Petite: I am 5' - 1", and almost always the

shortest person in the room. I suggest petite ladies like myself embrace monochrome ensembles - to create the illusion of length. Proportion is also key here, be careful to balance each garment and not overwhelm your small stature. Tucking in is recommended or belting a long blouse to give definition to your waist, are ways to achieve the illusion of length. And why not wear platform heels whenever possible? Best choices:

- maxi skirts

- all blouse shapes, with an emphasis on shorter length

Delightful Pears: Most of you lovelies out there have hips slightly larger than your upper body. Plan to draw more attention to the top part of your body with form-fitting tops, and a skimming hemline that will minimize your hip area. Best choices:

- A line skirts

- belted and fitted blouses andand tops

Sexy-Curvy: The hourglass girl. If you have lovely curves, your goal is to highlight them (not hide) by emphasizing your waist, which will flatter and celebrate your femininity. Best choices:

- A line skirts, belted jackets, cropped tops

Luscious Apple: You have a wide torso, broad shoulders, and a full bust, waist, and upper back.

A swingy top (narrow at the top, wider at the bottom) will easily flow over your midsection. Look for details that highlight your favorite parts of your body, like your shoulders, arms and legs for example. Reach for pieces and fabrics that add structure and a strong focal point up toward your face and shoulders. Best choices:

- cropped blazers

- peplum blouses and tops, create an illusion of a waist, and de-emphasis larger hips and stomach

Strong and Athletic: Sporty girls have many options. You may have strong shoulders and a thicker waist. Soften your straight shape and show off those assets with detailed tops that add more curve to your waist, and skirts that minimize a straighter midsection. **Best choices:**

- wrap tops, details that bring needed volume

- pencil and A line skirts

Blouses: The top 4:

1. Sleeveless blouse (also known as a shift) and camisoles: this shape is great for layering, either w/ adjustable thin straps, or no sleeves. A camisole hangs close to the body, an essential piece for warm climates.

2. Cap sleeve blouse: a small amount of fabric that cups the shoulder defines this shape. -This blouse is a layering basic and provides more coverage than sleeveless.

3. Long sleeve tunic: not just for bohemians, this shape can hide a thick middle. Choose one that is longer than your bottom to offer multiple styling opportunities.

4. Structured menswear shirting: a must have classic for the office or the opera. This shirt is the ultimate chameleon.

Blouse Silhouettes

1. Sleeveless shift &
Camisoles

2. Cap sleeve blouse

Blouse Silhouettes

3. Long sleeve tunic

4. Structured menswear shirting

Resource Guide:

Budget (around $30): H & M, Express, Simply Vera Wang for Kohl's

Mid-Range ($50 - $90): Zara, Lauren, Ralph Lauren, J. Crew, Splendid, Velvet, Top Shop, Banana Republic, Ann Taylor

Splurge (over $150): Theory, Joie, Vince, DVF, Trina Turk, Nanette Lepore

SECTION FOUR: Skirts - facts, tips and resources

Skirts: The top 4:

1. pencil skirt - a fitted classic, straight from the waist to hem, to the knee or mid-calf.

2. A-line skirt - most accommodating to all body shapes, small at the waist and moves out away from the body in an 'A" shape. Sometimes called a circle skirt, the hem should go to knee or mid-calf.

(Continued after pictures)

Skirt Silhouettes

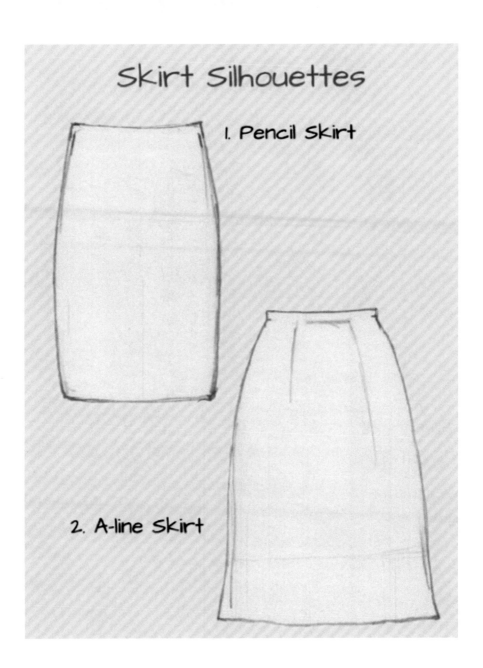

1. Pencil Skirt

2. A-line Skirt

Skirt Silhouettes

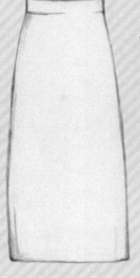

3. Column Maxi Skirt

4. Mini Skirt

3. column maxi skirt - easier to wear than you think, my favorite! Can be a straight or slightly A-line shape, hem goes to the floor.

4. mini -skirt - goes in andand out of popularity, shapes are straight, bell shape, hem goes anywhere from above the knee to mid-thigh

Resource Guide:

Budget ($30 - $50): Forever 21, Target, Express, Gap

Mid-Range ($70 - $100): J.Crew, Ann Taylor, Anthropology, Michael by Michael Kors

Splurge (over $150): Tibi, Rebecca Taylor, Alice and Olivia, Tory Burch, Theory, Tahari

Stylist tip:

In the Dressing room: Be adventurous, try on lots of styles to find the silhouette that fits and flatters your body. The good news is that with the abundance of designers on the market, there are many brands that make the ideal garments for you, flattering and comfortable. Be open to tailoring - add this very important resource to your budget.

SECTION FIVE: The Looks

Look 1: Start with A-line midi skirt and white camisole blouse.

Do you have the right lingerie?

I recommend a demi - cup, nude bra for underneath white, cream and sheer tops. A black T-shirt bra in a standard and racerback style are essentials as well.

Use this page to keep notes on what items you might need to buy to create these looks.

Look 2 - Blazing the Trail: Add a fitted black blazer and chunky jewelry - an ensemble fit for the office and cocktail hour.

What are kind of rules spoken or unspoken are still present in a traditional office setting?

Does this have an impact on what you choose to wear every day? Is it helpful or restricting?

Join my Facebook group and send me your questions : Be the Best You - Style Lab and I will enter you to win a V.I.P. styling package!

Accessories: Combine warm and cool neutrals here to complete your outfit. A classic Fendi baguette handbag fits easily under the arm, and you can never go wrong with heeled ankle boots. I found these Rag n' Bone booties - a cute name for 'ankle boot' on clearance at Nordstrom Rack. The zipper was broken, and I had my local shoe cobbler replace it for $20. Wow, this is one of my most famous deals of a lifetime!

Do you have one such shopping score?

Look 3- Headed to Brunch: Pair with a black silky tunic, silver fringe necklace and platform sandals.

If you are reading this book because you want to try wearing skirts more often, here is an idea: Give yourself an assignment to make an outfit like this one perhaps - and go to brunch!

Or head to a fancy coffee shop. Take a picture and paste it here, to start your own look-book!

Look 4 - Start with: Bold emerald, silk sleeveless blouse and pencil skirt. A tank top style blouse in silk is also a easy go - to top.

I like to have several sumptuous jewel tones in my closet to bring color to my face. Wearing all neutrals, or all black everyday can make you appear washed out, as black absorbs all color.

Wearing all black, everyday is not fashionable, it's a uniform. I understand that for some individuals, like Mark Zuckerberg, and many apparel designers, like Anna Sui and Vera Wang - there is a purpose, this uniformity in their clothes allows them to focus on their creative pursuit without distraction.

Wear color and start counting the compliments.

Look 5 - Free Spirit: Feel free to play with color and print. A floral skirt, paired with a dark denim jean jacket, studded leather cuff bracelet and crystal strand choker make a chic casual outfit.

As you afraid of prints? The easiest way to incorporate a print into your outfit, is to pull one or two colors, as we did with the green tank, and blue denim jacket - that are repeated in the floral print of the skirt.

Look 6 - Free Spirit II: A jean jacket can be left open, for comfort – as well as leaving the top untucked. The crystal necklace is left as a strand.

One of the most forgotten garments in your closet! A fitted, dark denim jean jacket can double as a blazer in a pinch, or a cover for a cocktail dress! The key here is the dark wash, and closely fitting silhouette. Artsy jewelry or an ornate chain detailed handbag are the needed extras to balance the feminine and the masculine vibe.

Do you need to be able to close all the buttons on a jacket? This is a common question. I say yes, with exception to the very top and very last buttons. If you disagree, send me a <u>Facebook</u> post or a tweet <u>@suzstyl</u> with the hashtags #denimjacket and #suzesstylelab - you will be entered to win a V.I.P. styling package.

Look 7 - Get Schooled: There is something about a pencil skirt and riding boots, that speaks to me about classic preppy styling. A doctor's bag is the perfect foil for our look. To complete the outfit, don a crystal necklace; it's become synonymous with Vogue magazine's Anna Wintour, the Queen of Style. To choker or not to choker, are you curious to try one, but worried you will be a throw back to the late 1980's? Weigh in here: Be the Best You - Style Lab

Look 8 - Ripple effect: A tasseled necklace adds edge to this look. Add classic accessories such as platform Prada sandals and a burgundy leather clutch, which read sophisticated and urban cool at the same time. A special thing about these Prada sandals, I found them at my local vintage shop Trends, in Oak Park, IL. Among the usual hodge-podge of clothes and accessories, they have a luxury -designer shoe and garment rack. I literally run in there every month or so and riffle through... you never know what you will find! Do you shop at resale shops - if not, why not?

Look 9 - Start with: Green silk sleeveless blouse paired with a denim maxi skirt. This skirt is from Free People. It's hard to resist their brand of cool girl stuff!

Look 10 - Shangri-La Chic: A denim maxi skirt is your new best friend. Try this instead of jeans then pair with your bold jewel tone blouse (like my green one here) and my favorite layering pieces: a kimono.

I heard this quote once 'Big clothes open doors.' I love that, because when you present yourself well, you are treated better - not just by others, but how you think about and treat yourself!

Here is your homework: make an outfit inspired by this look and attach it here!

The Extras: a menswear watch is the star here. A delicate necklace keeps green crystal pendant earrings in balance, and a large turquoise ring ties this set of accessories together. What accessories might you be missing? Use this this page to keep notes on what items you need to create similar ensembles of your own.

Look 11 - Start with: White camisole blouse paired with a denim maxi skirt.

I asked before if you have the right lingerie, is is comfortable and useful? I recommended a demi - cup, nude bra for underneath white, cream and sheer tops.

Where do you shop for bras and underwear? Here is my new favorite way to shop for underpinnings - online! Check out the selection of MAJAMAS: Suze's Style Lab Shop & Peach Bras here:

Mimi Sagadin
www.discoverpeach.com/s/mimis

Look 12 -La Boehme: Add a tassel pendant necklace and fringe trimmed sheer vest, platform sandals = perfect strolling outfit.

A caftan is another bohemian obsession of mine. I imagine myself lounging by the famous Moroccan patio of Yves St. Laurent. Very 1960's CHIC!

Do you have Fashion Icons from the past or modern day who inspire your style? Let me know - Instagram: #styleicon

Look 13 - Guilt Complex: Captivate in chic separates by adding a sequined bomber jacket and trade bead strand necklace! Speaking of Style Icons, there are many who influence me. One of my most beloved is famous New York Interior and Fashion Designer, Iris Apfel. "More is more and less is a bore."

The Extras: a casual -cool mix of accessories here are reflective of a street style that is easy to pull off. A tasseled pendant necklace and beaded tribal cuff are the stars. Combine with lady - like sandals, clutch handbag and classic menswear watch. These are an uplifting compliment to the most basic of blouse and skirt outfits.

There are those Prada sandals again. When you find the perfect shoe you worship it. The Movado watch, by the way, was a gift to my husband from his Mother - its very precious, I wear it frequently, and it makes me happy.

Look 14 - Vintage Central: Another amazing look with denim maxi skirt, beaded onyx and pyrite necklace and vintage long cardigan from Missoni.

Send me your outfit pix to my <u>Facebook</u> or Instagram, <u>@suzstyl</u> with the hashtags #vintagecardigan and #suzesstylelab - you could win a V.I.P. styling package. oh ya…

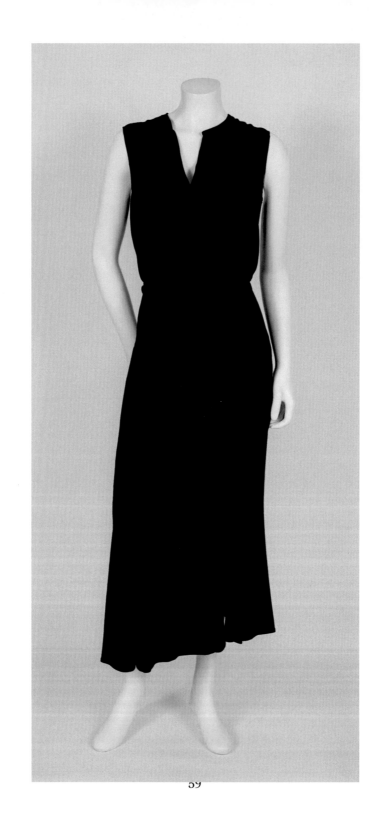

Look 15 - Start with: navy sleeveless tunic and charcoal knit maxi skirt.

My friend Shernette made this amazing grey knit skirt for me! A finalist on Toronto's Project Runway, Shernette Swaby creates beautifully hand tailored (here in Chicago) garments for all body shapes - perfect for work, play and travel. I reach for her clothes almost every day.

Look 16 - Instagramable: Effortless style at its best by adding a silk tasseled scarf and leather cuff bracelets.

Scarves: pair w/ anything in need of a twist or a spot of color at your face. I haven't counted lately, but I probably have about 30 scarves in my rotation. I wear them as a shawl, in my hair, around my neck, as a belt, the list goes on. I always have a rotating selection of scarves in my Suze's Style Lab Shop.

Versatile embellishments: Flat mules are a smart shoe choice for day to evening. The mules pictured here are vintage fabric and velvet from Stuart Weitzman. True love.

Include an extra-long knotted strand of faceted - agate and metallic beads. Also, one can never go wrong with a huge Buddha ring. Try it!

Look 17 - Instagramable BOOST: Pair a maroon cardigan and coordinating silk scarf for a flowing silhouette. Pull it all together with an architectural satchel - my favorite style of handbag. No matter how relaxed your look is, a sharp handbag can be the glue for any outfit.

Here is an idea: create an ensemble inspired by this look and attach it here; then wear it to coffee with your girlfriends. Send it to me and be featured in one of my newsletters or Facebook posts.

Look 18 - Start with: Classic white shirt and A-line mini skirt. This shape skirt is super flattering as it created an exaggerated small waistline. The graphic pattern is so fun, it makes me happy.

Look 19 - the Wild one: Challenge yourself with the ultimate masculine-feminine contrast, by combining a camel color moto-jacket and graphic print mini skirt.

I will always wear tights with a short skirt. It just makes for clean lines, and if you happen to have a few veins or any other unwanted attributes. Stretchy tights or fishnets will cover all flaws. Additionally, I will only wear tights that do NOT have control top…those are the devil.

Check out my <u>Suze's Style Lab Shop.</u> where I have a rotating selection of tights.

Look 20 - Pattern Play: Switch out the jacket for a scarf in floral -animal print.

There is a nice balance with the scale of the 2 prints: the scarf is small and the skirt is medium-large. When combining prints, keep this in mind.

Are you keeping track of your outfits here?

Look 21- Caped Crusade: Never boring, a cape is a must-have for the cooler seasons.

Remember, your outerwear - coats - need to be equally curated. This is where you make a first impression; so choose wisely, and have several in your line-up.

If you are in the camp of 'Hell no, I will NEVER wear a cape,' tell me why!

Send an email: suzesolari@me.com

Look 22 - Start with: - Chambray blouse and a classic' LBS' little black (A-line) skirt. Soft can be chic. Cozy can be confident - try something new, and wear your weekend chambray shirt with an office ready skirt.

Get more milage from your wardrobe by mixing things up and making 'new' outfits from your closet. Keep your options open and have FUN.

Look 23 - The Lovely Bones: A-line skirt and chambray blouse, leather and gold chain belt and choker necklace complete the look.

A frilly jacket would finish things off here. Send a pic of yourself in a similar outfit to my Facebook or tweet @suzstyl with the hashtags #denimshirt and #suzesstylelab - enter to win a prize.

Look 24 – Role Model: Adding a sweater vest is comfy chic at its best! How cute is this vest from Anthropology?

Vest are indispensable for securing a cute, finished look; as well as adding a layer of warmth.. this is a styling trick I do often.

Look 25 - Start with: Chambray button down blouse and A-line midi skirt. The plaid pattern on this skirt and tulle lining is super feminine. I enjoy the richness of contrasting this type of skirt with a masculine blouse on top.

Walk TALL: an over the knee suede, boot would be another way to achieve this contrast.

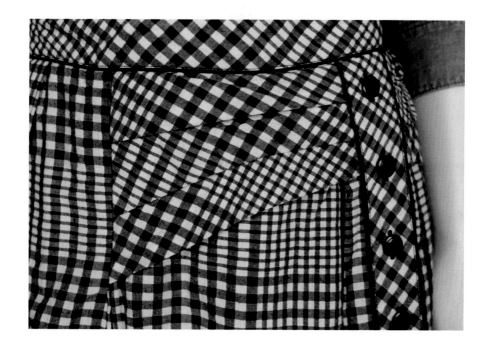

Add ons, the Silver Standard: Silver metal fringed necklace – this is one my FAVORITES, it's from Stella and Dot, and its so cool.

In general, I like to pair silver jewelry with cool colors and neutrals: grey, black, blues and purples.

Look 26 –Dressed Up Denim: just add jewelry, an A-line Midi skirt is ultra-flattering for every body type.

Funny thing about this picture: I meant to layer a black leather jacket over the shoulders to finish the look. Did I run out of time ? ...photo shoots are EXHAUSTING! Just imagine one here.

I have MANY leather jackets, they are super versatile as transitional, season outerwear, or as an inside layer. My favorite one is a BCBG black leather moto-style, jacket from Nordstrom Rack.

Stylist tip:

One of my favorite tricks to extending my wardrobe and
utilizing pieces in NEW ways is to wear a dress as a
tunic. Pair with skinny jeans or leggings, and poof – you
have a 'new' outfit without having to go shopping.

SECTION SIX: Accessories

As I have said before: accessorizing your outfit is not only highly encouraged – it's in this process that you discover your personal style aesthetic, showing who you are as an individual, in the truest expression of you! Accessories have transformative power beyond anything else in your closet. In the <u>T-Shirt and Jeans Handbook</u>, I go into detail about what are the basic accessories, the must-have's, that allow you to finish many outfits.

My 25 years in the interior design industry and vast experience mixing colors, patterns and textures has informed and influenced the strategies I use and share with you here to create and finish your outfits.

Jewelry:

When it comes to jewelry, I am a self -confessed "more is more addict." I am very SHINY! And like to wear lots of jewelry at once, making thoughtful selections that layer like sculpture.

Jewelry is a personal thing, and you've got to experiment to find a balance that works with your own style. That said, going completely unadorned misses the opportunity to say something about your individuality! I encourage you to wear a few pieces of jewelry to elevate your look every day.

In 'the Looks' section I have shown you how to incorporate jewelry into your Blouse and Skirt outfits.

General Jewelry Tips:

I want to address the question of mixing metals with jewelry. The secret is to mix 2 or more metals in the same area, such as gold and silver bracelets stacked together. Choosing pieces with several metals in the design is an easy way to accomplish this. If you wear gold earrings and a silver necklace, the eye will notice the imbalance; it's a small detail but one worth paying attention to.

Proportion: think about the layout of your jewelry choices, and how they are balanced, just like how paint is applied to a canvas in a portrait. Where do you want to draw the viewers eye? Pair large earrings with more delicate necklaces and vice versa. The same theory applies to statement rings and thinner bracelets.

Layer a few small necklaces to make one cohesive look. For another layering trick, try wearing several delicate necklace with various lengths; it's a proportion thing really that works. Experiment with a combination of metals, beaded stones, leather, whatever says 'YOU'.

Top Must haves:
Necklaces:
- dainty and bold
Bracelets:
-tiny, one at a time, or layered.
-big and bold: cuffs, or a huge, assorted stack

Earrings:

- Studs: diamond and semi -precious stones.

– Hoops: never go out of style.

– Chandeliers: stunning for night and day. I wear my dangling darlings, for instant "cool", added to a striped top and distressed jeans!

Rings: A striking accessory, rings are eternal, a symbol of love, commitment – and can be handed down through the generations.

I'm always in support of large cocktail rings, just one can carry your whole outfit. Or try stacking a few for a new look!

Stylist tip:

How do you get a knot out of a fine chain? I had this
problem recently, and discovered a way to save myself a
trip to the jeweler. Here is what you need: olive oil and a
fine pointed metal implement, such as beading awl or you
can use a safety pin. A few drops of the oil on the knot
will lubricate the chain enough for you to pry the knot
apart w/ the awl – et voile!

SHOES, a Love story:

The effort you put into assembling a smart outfit can be squandered, if you add the wrong footwear. Finding comfortable and stylish shoes is very much possible. You just should search, and spend a bit more. Almost every woman I know can describe the agony of buying an inexpensive shoe and regretting it. The best way of inspecting quality is the fit and materials. The pattern of a shoe, the construction and fit in the toe box and ankle are as important as the materials. Vinyl and fabric are the hallmark of cheap shoes, and potentially will not provide the comfort and lasting qualities of leather.

High-quality shoes and boots are worth the investment, and so are you! In my first book, I gave quite a lot of detail on which shoes I recommend as the basics. I will review them for you here, and describe which skirt hem lengths are best paired with each shoe type. Also included is my resources guide for where to find them and at what price points.

4 TOP Categories: Find your SOLE Mate(s)

FLATS: Sneakers, loafers, ballet flats. Maxi and mini -

skirts are the best skirt length the pair with flats.

HEELS: Stacked heels, platform pumps and Mary Janes. Midi-skirts in pencil or A-line are most flattering paired w/ heels.

SANDALS: Platform and wedge. You are good to go with all skirt types, with exception to mini's. Use caution here ... I recommend wearing flat sandals w/ mini -skirts. The short length of the skirt is the main event. If you were to also wear heels, you have a competing dynamic, and risk showing a bit too much leg. A subtle and stylish look is to pair with flat shoes.

BOOTS: Block heel ankle booties, tall heel and riding boots. I adore all BOOTS! Skirt hems can be paired with boots to create chic and comfortable outfits. Just make sure the hem of your midi or mini doesn't hit the same height as the boot, slightly higher or lower will look best. Try an open-toe option for spring / summer.

SHOE and BOOT Resource Guide:

Budget ($50 - $100): Nicole, Gap, Born, Dolce Vita, Steve Madden

Mid-Range ($100 - $150): Dansko, Olu Kai, Birkenstock Birki's, Earthie's, Sam Edelman, Naot, Naya by Naturalizer, Kork - Ease, Vince Camuto

Splurge (over $200): Frye, Free Bird by Free People, Aquatilia, Picolino's, Ash, DVF, Coach, Michael Kors

Handbags:

If there is a weakness for accessories, mine would have to

be handbags – purses, or pocket books, as my clients in Boston refer to them. I think of them as friends and take care to store and clean the leather bags with a moisturizing oil treatment once a year.

The fabric covers are useful, stuffed with tissue to create an insert; this helps preserve the shape.

Building a handbag collection can be easy and fun. Be strategic, and think long term: consider the quality of materials andand your lifestyle. These Top 3 types of handbags will cover any event and are highly functional. If you have space and budget to invest in more, by all means, go for it – keep in mind that handbags are a reflection of where we are in our life, ie: how many Kate Spade diaper bags do you really need? Also, your handbag selection should reflect the theme or aesthetic of your outfit. For example, a fancy skirt detailed in lace or sequins calls for a polished clutch, not a canvas messenger bag. And remember, quality always wins out over quantity. One more suggestion – avoid black lining in your handbags – a deep dark hole making finding keys impossible.

Top 3 Handbags:

Satchel or Doctor's bag

Evening bag or Clutch

Cross-body Tote

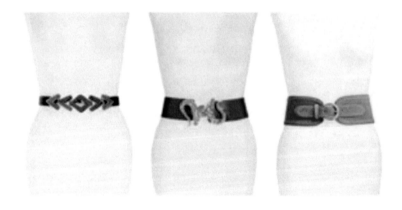

Belts:

This accessory is not only the most commonly missing
piece from my client's closet, but has the power to
complete and transform every outfit. Why do so many of

us neglect belts? 'I have no waist' is the comment I usually hear.

The fact is, a belt will highlight the smallest part of our plus size bodies and will create a curvy figure for our boyish shaped sisters. A belt can also be the binding component for completing a blouse and skirt look, melding color and texture. Also, consider how belting a longer blouse pulls in the volume, creating a new silhouette. Paired with leather or faux leather leggings, a belted dress is now a tunic!

Top 2 Belts:

-Thin: in black and brown leather or leopard (my new neutral) if you can invest in one of these w/ silver and gold metal, you are all set.

-Medium width: for placing on the waist, with a stretchy elastic is comfy and a perfect finish to skirts with a tucked in blouse.

Sunglasses, top 3:

-The Aviator

-Wayfarers

-Round Oversized

Did I already say I had an addiction to accessories? My love of sunglasses surpasses that of most people, but I have very good reasons to possess many of these fabulous essentials! My eyes are blue, and sensitive to a bright day.

I swear that years of wearing lovely Sunnies w/ UVA – UVB protection has saved me from wrinkles around my eyes; function and form, what could be better? You can't go wrong with these classic styles that look good on almost every face shape.

Section Take Aways

1. Accessories are KEY to completing every outfit. Having these highly person pieces at the ready are

indispensable to saving you time, and encouraging your creativity.

2. Don't skimp: invest time and cash to finding comfortable and chic shoes.

3. Choose your handbags wisely; marry form and function, and have some fun!

4. Choose at least one accessory that says who you are and gives you a focal point for your outfit.

SECTION SEVEN: Expert Style Tips and How To's

Now that you have the knowledge and inspiration to bring out your skirts and wear them with confidence, let's go through some helpful ways to revolutionize your routine, create new habits and find your style with blouses, skirts and more:

How to Shop - the Secret to shopping

It is my belief that if we are equipped with the right tools in the dressing room, we make less purchasing mistakes and therefore have a more organized, efficient and inspiring closet.

I enjoy the high-street stores for their affordable prices that allow us to try out new trends without a major commitment. But in addition to of-the-moment wares, these shops can produce great staples you can wear for multiple seasons. Keep a close eye on quality, however, and use these tips to make the most informed purchase.

Fiber content: does the fabric feel good? This is one of the most important factors to determine whether something is worth buying. Think in terms of longevity, and investment. When shopping at affordable stores, opt for materials that look and feel luxe. For example, satins and silks tend to look more expensive. If it feels synthetic, pass it by.

Questions to ponder:

1. Does It Fit Me Properly?

Many cheaper brands skimp on fit, resulting in poor proportions and inconsistent sizing. When you're trying on blouses, make sure it fits in the arms, shoulders, bust. Skirts should lay flat on your waist and skim your hips. If you have to spend extra money for alterations, it may be not be worth it. Conversely, if you have a good tailor you can have alterations to garments to better suit your body and make something that looks good –look great with a few tweaks.

2. How often will I wear it?

Ask: Is this a trend that will likely move on in one season? An asymmetrical skirt for example, or high – low blouse. Is this a bold print that you might grow tired of? You should have pieces that are fun, make a statement and that you can make multiple outfits with it.

3. Do I have many similar items like this already in my closet? Before you check out or hit 'pay', do this critical edit. Super affordable prices or sales can sometimes make us go a little crazy. I have a client who pulled out 20 white blouses from her closet. Nobody needs that many white blouses! Duplicates take up valuable real estate in your closet, providing countless options, lending to the state I call 'the overwhelm'. Additionally, too many of one item could indicate a shopping addiction and feeling of guilt over whether or not you should have bought those items. There is nothing so necessary that it should cause you financial, or emotional distress.

4. Speaking in financial terms, do you plan a budget before you go out to shop? Prepare a shopping list for the items missing from your closet. If you stick to your budget, you are more likely to return home with only the

items you truly need.

Remember, a tightly edited wardrobe results in a more refined reflection of the true nature of your style aesthetic and a collection of genuinely flattering clothes.

If you think less is more, you share the strategy of European women. Instead of stuffing your closet with mediocre pieces, shop smart and learn how to choose elevated higher quality options. Make sure you ask these crucial questions before you purchase.

HOW TO Pack: for Travel and Work

Not sure what to pack for vacation or a business trip? Or maybe you are like most of us, and you habitually over pack. I believe that we all want to feel like a million bucks when we travel, and enjoy our trips so much more when we do.

Also, whether you're packing for a short weekend getaway or trying to avoid fees for checked luggage, knowing how to strategically pack carry-on luggage is an essential skill to have.

Be empowered to create outfits that suit your style and be

fully prepared for your trips with this packing protocol and ensure you have these basic pieces in your wardrobe.

Protocol:

You want to feel comfortable and be stylish too, so the first thing to do is review the activities and events in your itinerary, and make lists of what to pack. I always do this, even laying out the outfits, together with accessories to ensure I pack precisely what I need. It is wise to think in terms of layers for almost any trip, especially locations with cool and wet climates.

Think about a main 'color story' and work off that. For example, you may want to go with a brown pallet as your main neutral. Brown and tan tones for all accessories: shoes, boots, sandals, belts; then warm tones for clothing: orange, yellow, tans and reds as colors for tops. A medium to dark rinse for jeans, white and khakis for bottoms. Gold tone jewelry goes best with a brown in general, and toss in a few silk scarves. Scarves are super handy for bad hair days, instant change up of your outfits, and for warmth!

Or, you could choose Black instead - so all shoes, handbags are black or have black in them. Then go with a cool pallet: blues, navy, greens, purples ... any kind of jeans, white too, for bottoms. Silver accessories are best w/ black. You can put grey into each of these 'color stories', keeping prints simple and to a minimum for ease of combining garments to make multiple outfits.

I always wrap my silky blouses and delicates in a sealed garment bag. This step not only protects them from the contents in your suitcase, but keeps wrinkles at bay. One more thing: always bring a maxi skirt, indispensable for creating a casual or dressy outfit!

Check these articles out too:
http://chicago.racked.com/2013/11/15/7637037/a-tsafriendly-outfit-from-stylist-suze-solari#4466410
http://www.refinery29.com/travel-clothes

HOW TO Layer: the Art form of Layering

I love to think of the body as a pallet. Why not think of building your outfit in the same way a painter would add to a canvas, in stages. This dressing concept is useful not only in fall and winter, but all year round.

Transitioning from summer and early fall into the colder season, I am frequently asked what to wear that will keep one warm in the morning, but flexible enough to change it in the afternoon? It can be challenging to find basics that are stylish and warm, and provide maximum outfit creating potential.

The answer is layers. Easy pieces that provide a foundation for our everyday wardrobe. We can use these magical items to build a multitude of outfits, and extend our warmer weather items throughout the year.

Camisole and sleeveless blouses in neutral colors are a perfect base for layering because they hold their shape and provide a blank canvas for building numerous outfits. Combine these with long, draped cardigans, fur and knit sweater vests. These blouses are also perfect for layering under a structured blazer or jean jacket for day; throw on a sequined cardigan or a chunky necklace and you are ready for a glamorous night out. I reach for capes year-round, and enjoy wearing one over a leather jacket for added warmth and panache on colder days.

A little insight about layers: with enough of these pieces, you need not fully distinguish between winter and summer seasons.

With exception to a few items such a fur and heavy woolen garments and heavy tall boots, my wardrobe doesn't change much from each season. Not only do I save the time and energy of not moving my entire closet around twice a year, this practice keeps clutter down, ensuring I love and wear everything in my closet.

HOW TO: stay organized & save time in your closet

SLIDESHOW

Keep your closet updated and organized, so you can easily and quickly get dressed in style and comfort every day:

1. Reign in excess - remove items that are the wrong size, fit or disrepair, and pieces that don't bring you JOY.

2. Update your space: a fresh coat of paint, an area rug and full length mirror are simple touches creating an oasis inspiring you every day.

3. Invest in organizing tools: a valet hook for staging

outfits; a jewelry rack and Bangle Stacker for keeping necklaces, bracelets and earring displayed in an orderly way, so you can find everything and wear them.

HOW TO: care for your skirt and blouses

-How often should you dry clean your skirts and blouses? Dry cleaning breaks down the integrity of the fibers, so I recommend hand washing with diluted liquid detergent and hang drying. Skirts can be worn MANY times before they need to be cleaned, just spot clean stains with lemon juice or a detergent pen for spots. Lemon juice is great for keeping whites white too!

- Store skirts on hangers with clips and blouses on thin flocked hangers with a generous curve to the 'arms', preventing shoulder nipples on your tops. I recommend organizing by color, from light to dark, in a rainbow pattern. This makes spotting each item easier; this is a huge time saver, also making outfit building more creative.

HOW TO: implement new habits for success

-make your own digital look book. Assemble entire outfits, including accessories, shoes, and handbag; then take pictures of your outfits and create a photo gallery.

- Establish a routine – maybe you decide what you will wear for the week, and set out each outfit the night before.

- Get your girlfriend's onboard. Set up an accountability group to encourage each other and share 'new outfit' pics.

Buy a copy of this book for friends – when you share your ideas you empower not just yourself but inspire others to transform their lives too!

- Join my facebook community: <u>Be the Best YOU, Style Lab</u>

- <u>Stop in frequently to my online boutique, where I have a rotating collection of blouses, skirts, accessories and layering pieces to create and maintain a fabulous wardrobe: Suze's Style Lab Shop</u>

-Practice these steps and create new and empowering habits. These simple, time saving steps will change your behavior and improve the quality of your life.

Thank You Page:

With Gratitude & Appreciation

To my lovely Readers whose reviews & suggestions were the inspiration for this book.

To my favorite Artist & Graphic designer, for the cover design:
Christy Smith: # 708-267-1699 http://christysmithartist.com/

To my Inspirational & Spiritual Business Coach:
Kelly Sheets: http://kellysheets.com/

To my Strategic Business Coach:
Amy Latzen Birks: http://hustlefreebusiness.com/

To my lovely Photographer: Eileen Molony. http://www.emphotography.net/

To my amazing husband Joe Solari: for tech support, formatting, editing & publishing. Find out what is available for you in self-publishing: http://

About the Author

Suze Solari is a Professional stylist & award winning Fashion writer. Suze grew up in Portland, Oregon, a town where style wasn't part of the culture. The third of five kids, she wore hand-me-downs and parochial school uniforms. However, her great aunt's treasure trove of jewelry and fur coats captured her interest, and a stylist was born.

Her first book, The T Shirt & Jeans Handbook, was written for women who have lost their style and want it back. An easy to follow resource and look-book for upgrading your daily uniform.

She is known for helping her clients achieve their own personal style to suit their lifestyle, and maximize their wardrobe investment, by mixing and matching existing pieces in new ways.

Her philosophy is that your closet should promote joy,

empowerment and confidence. Suze serves clients in Chicago, L.A., Portland OR, Austin TX, Atlanta, Boston & Connecticut. You can learn more about Suze at www.suzesolaristyle.com.

TEXT Blouse to 44222 and get bonus video content and flat lays for FREE!

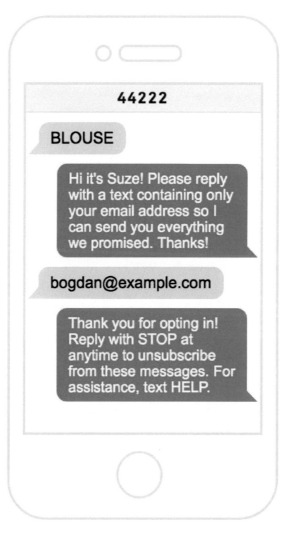

20613668R00076

Made in the USA
Lexington, KY
05 December 2018